The True Confession of George Barker

THE
TRUE
CONFESSION
OF
GEORGE
BARKER

By George Barker

NEW AMERICAN LIBRARY

821.91

B255t

FIRST PRINTING

Published by The New American Library of World Literature, Inc.
501 Madison Avenue, New York, New York 10022

Published simultaneously in Canada
by The New American Library
of Canada Limited, Toronto, Ontario

Library of Congress Catalog Card Number: 64–15730
Printed in the United States of America

Designed by Klaus Gemming

210695

I suppose it's possible that we forget
    The things we'd rather that we never
Ever remembered, but, although we're very clever,
    We're really not all that clever, yet.
When I call devils from the deep
    The damned brutes answer only too pronto,
Skipping up out of the beds of sleep
    Not at my call, but because they want to.

Rome 1962

BOOK I

1

TODAY, recovering from influenza,
　　I begin, having nothing worse to do,
This autobiography that ends a
　　Half of my life I'm glad I'm through.
O Love, what a bloody hullaballoo
　　I look back at, shaken and sober,
When that intemperate life I view
　　From this temperate October.

To nineteen hundred and forty-seven
　　I pay the deepest of respects,
For during this year I was given
　　Some insight into the other sex.
I was a victim, till forty-six,
　　Of the rosy bed with bitches in it;
But now, in spite of all pretexts,
　　I never sleep a single minute.

O fellow sailor on the tossing sea,
　　O fleeting virgin in the night,
O privates, general in lechery,
　　Shun, shun the bedroom like a blight:
Evade, O amorous acolyte,
　　That pillow where your heart you bury—
For if the thing was stood upright
　　It would become a cemetery.

I start with this apostrophe
　　To all apostles of true love:
With your devotion visit me,
　　Give me the glory of the dove

That dies of dereliction. Give
　　True love to me, true love to me,
And in two shakes I will prove
　　It's false to you and false to me.

Bright spawner, on your sandbank dwell
　　Coldblooded as a plumber's pipe—
The procreatory ocean swell
　　Warming, till they're overripe,
The cockles of your cold heart, will
　　Teach us true love can instil
Temperature into any type.

Does not the oyster in its bed
　　Open a yearning yoni when
The full moon passes overhead
　　Feeling for pearls? O nothing, then,
Too low a form of life is, when
　　Love, abandoning the cloister,
Can animate the bedded oyster,
　　The spawning tiddler, and men.

Thus all of us, the pig and prince,
　　The priest and the psychiatrist,
Owe everything to true love, since
　　How the devil could we exist
If our parents had never kissed?
　　All biographies, therefore,
—No matter what else they evince—
　　Open, like prisons, with adore.

Remember, when you love another,
    Who demonstrably is a bitch,
Even Venus had a mother
    Whose love, like a silent aitch,
Incepted your erotic itch.
    Love, Love has the longest history,
For we can tell an ape his father
    Begot him on a mystery.

I, born in Essex thirty-four
    Essentially sexual years ago,
Stepped down, looked around, and saw
    I had been cast a little low
In the social register
    For the friends whom I now know.
Is a constable a mister?
    Bob's your uncle, even so.

Better men than I have wondered
    Why one's father could not see
That at one's birth he had blundered.
    His ill-chosen paternity
Embarrasses the fraternity
    Of one's friends who, living Huysmans,[1]
Understandably have wondered
    At fatherhood permitted policemen.

So I, the son of an administer
    Of the facts of civil laws,
Delight in uncivil and even sinister
    Violations. Thus my cause
Is simply, friend, to hell with yours.
    In misdemeanours I was nourished—
Learnt, like altruists in Westminster,
    By what duplicities one flourished.

At five, but feeling rather young,
     With a blue eye beauty over six,
Hand in hand and tongue to tongue
     I took a sin upon my sex.
Sin? It was pleasure. So I told her.
     And ever since, persisting in
Concupiscences no bolder,
     My pleasure's been to undress sin.

What's the point of a confession
     If you have nothing to confess?
I follow the perjuring profession
     —O poet, lying to impress!—
But the beautiful lie in a beautiful dress
     Is the least heinous of my transgressions:
When a new one's added, "O who was it?"
     Sigh the skeletons in my closet.

Ladybird, ladybird, come home, come home:
     Muse and mistress, wherever you are.
The evening is here and in the gloom
     Each bisexual worm burns like a star
And the love of man is crepuscular.
     In the day the world. But, at night, we,
Lonely on egoes dark and far
     Apart as worlds, between sea and sea,

Yearn on each other as the stars hold
     One another in fields together.
O rose of all the world, enfold
     Each weeping worm against the cold
Of the bitter ego's weather:
     To warm our isothermal pride
Cause, sometimes, Love, another
     To keep us by an unselfish side.

The act of human procreation
    —The rutting tongue, the grunt and shudder,
The sweat, the reek of defecation,
    The cradle hanging by the bladder,
The scramble up the hairy ladder,
    And from the thumping bed of Time
Immortality, a white slime,
    Sucking at its mother's udder—

The act of human procreation
    —The sore dug plugging, the lugged-out bub,
The small man priming a lactation,
    The grunt, the drooping teat, the rub
Of gum and dug, the slobbing kiss:
    Behold the mater amabilis,
Sow with a saviour, messiah and cow,
    Virgin and piglet, son and sow:—

The act of human procreation,
    —O crown and flower, O culmination
Of perfect love throughout creation—
    What can I compare to it?
O eternal butterflies in the belly,
O trembling of the heavenly jelly,
O miracle of birth! Really
    We are excreted, like shit.

2

THE Church, mediatrix between heaven
    And human fallibility,
Reminds us that the age of seven
    Inaugurates the Reason we
Spend our prolonged seniority
    Transgressing. Of that time I wish
I could recount a better story
    Than finding a shilling and a fish.

But Memory flirts with seven veils
    Peekabooing the accidental;
And what the devil it all entails
    Only Sigmund Freud suspects.
I think my shilling and my fish
    Symbolized a hidden wish
To sublimate these two affects:
    Money is nice and so is sex.

The Angel of Reason, descending
    On my seven-year-old head
Inscribed this sentence by my bed:
    The pleasure of money is unending
But sex satisfied is sex dead.
    I tested to see if sex died
But, all my effort notwithstanding,
    Have never found it satisfied.

Abacus of Reason, you have been
    The instrument of my abuse,
The North Star I have never seen,
    The trick for which I have no use:
The Reason, gadget of schoolmasters,
    Pimp of the spirit, the smart aleck,
Proud engineer of disasters,
    I see phallic: you, cephalic.

Happy those early days when I
    Attended an elementary school
Where seven hundred infant lives
    Flittered like gadflies on the stool
(We discovered that contraceptives
    Blown up like balloons, could fly) ;
We memorized the Golden Rule:
    Lie, lie, lie, lie.

For God's sake, Barker. This is enough
    Regurgitated obscenities,
Whimsicalities and such stuff.
    Where's the ineffable mystery,
The affiancing to affinities
    Of the young poet? The history
Of an evolving mind's love
    For the miseries and the humanities?

The sulking and son-loving Muse
    Grabbed me when I was nine. She saw
It was a question of self-abuse
    Or verses. I tossed off reams before
I cared to recognize their purpose.
    While other urchins were blowing up toads
With pipes of straw stuck in the arse,
    So was I, but I also wrote odes.

There was a priest, a priest, a priest,
    A Reverend of the Oratory,
Who taught me history. At least
    He taught me the best part of his story.
  Fat Father William, have you ceased
    To lead boys up the narrow path
Through the doors of the Turkish Bath?
    I hope you're warm in Purgatory.

And in the yard of the tenement
    —The Samuel Lewis Trust—I played
While my father, for the rent
    (Ten bob a week and seldom paid),
Trudged London for a job. I went
    Skedaddling up the scanty years,
My learning, like the rent, in arrears,
    But sometimes making the grade.

O boring kids! In spite of Freud
    I find my childhood recollections
Much duller now than when I enjoyed
    It. The whistling affections,
All fitting wrong, toy railway sections
    Running in circles. Cruel as cats
Even the lower beasts avoid
    These inhumanitarian brats.

Since the Age of Reason's seven
    And most of one's friends over eight,
Therefore they're reasonable? Even
    Sensible Stearns or simpleton Stephen
Wouldn't claim that. I contemplate
    A world which, at crucial instants,
Surrenders to adulterant infants
    The adult onus to think straight.

At the bottom of this murky well
    My childhood, like a climbing root,
Nursed in dirt the simple cell
    That pays itself this sour tribute.
Track any poet to a beginning
    And in a dark room you discover
A little boy intent on sinning
    With an etymological lover.

I peopled my youth with the pulchritude
    Of heterae noun-anatomized;
The literature that I prized
    Was anything to do with the nude
Spirit of creative art
    Who whispered to me: "Don't be queasy.
Simply write about a tart
    And there she is. The rest's easy."

And thus, incepted in congenial
    Feebleness of moral power
I became a poet. Venial
    As a human misdemeanour,
Still, it gave me, prisoner
    In my lack of character,
Pig to the Circean Muse's honour.
    Her honour? Why, it's lying on her.

Dowered, invested and endowed
    With every frailty is the poet—
Yielding to wickedness because
    How the hell else can he know it?
The tempted poet must be allowed
    All ethical latitude. His small flaws
Bring home to him, in sweet breaches,
    The moral self-indulgence teaches.

Where was I? Running, so to speak,
   To the adolescent seed? I
Found my will power rather weak
   And my appetites rather greedy

About the year of the General Strike,
   So I struck, as it were, myself:
Refused to do anything whatsoever, like
   Exercise books on a shelf.

Do Youth and Innocence prevail
   Over that cloudcuckoo clime
Where the seasons never fail
   And the clocks forget the time?
Where the peaks of the sublime
   Crown every thought; where every vale
Has its phantasy and phantasm
   And every midnight its orgasm?

I mooned into my fourteenth year
   Through a world pronouncing harsh
Judgments I could not quite hear
   About my verse, my young moustache
And my bad habits. In Battersea Park
   I almost heard strangers gossip
About my poems, almost remark
   The bush of knowledge on my lip.

Golden Calf, Golden Calf, where are you now
   Who lowed so mournfully in the dense
Arcana of my adolescence?
   No later anguish of bull or cow
Could ever be compared with half
   The misery of the amorous calf
Moonstruck in moonshine. How could I know
   You can't couple Love with any sense?

Poignant as a swallowed knife,
 Abstracted as a mannequin,
Remote as music, touchy as skin,
 Apotheosizing life
Into an apocalypse,
 Young Love, taking Grief to wife,
And tasting the bitterness of her lips,
 Forgets it comes from swabbing gin.

The veils descend. The unknown figure
 Is sheeted in the indecencies
Of shame and boils. The nose gets bigger.
 The private parts, haired like a trigger,
Cock at a dream. The infant cries
 Abandoned in its discarded larva,
Out of which steps, with bloodshot eyes,
 The man, the man, crying Ave, Ave!

3

THAT Frenchman[2] really had the trick
    Of figure skating in this stanza:
But I, thank God, cannot read Gallic
    And so escape his influenza.
Above my head his rhetoric
    Asks emulation. I do not answer.
It is as though I had not heard
    Because I cannot speak a word.

But I invoke him, dirty dog,
    As one barker to another:
Lift over me your clever leg,
    Teach me, you snail-swallowing frog,
To make out of a spot of bother
    Verses that shall catalogue
Every exaggerated human claim,
    Every exaggerated human aim.

I entreat you, frank villain,
    Get up out of your bed of dirt
And guide my hand. You are still an
    Irreprehensible expert
At telling Truth she's telling lies.
    Get up, liar; get up, cheat,
Look the bitch square in the eyes
    And you'll see what I entreat.

We share, frog, much the same well.
    I sense your larger spectre down
Here among the social swill
    Moving at ease beside my own
And the muckrakers I have known.
    No, not the magnitude I claim
That makes your shade loom like a tall
    Memorial but the type's the same.

You murdered with a knife, but I
    Like someone out of Oscar Wilde
Commemorate with a child
    The smiling victims as they die
Slewing in kisses and the lie
    Of generation. But we both killed.
I rob the grave you glorify,
    You glorify where I defiled.

O most adult adulterer
    Preside, now, coldly, over
My writing hand, as to it crowd
    The images of those unreal years
That, like a curtain, seem to stir
    Guiltily over what they cover—
Those unreal years, dreamshot and proud,
    When the vision first appears.

The unveiled vision of all things
    Walking towards us as we stand
And giving us, in either hand,
    The knowledge that the world brings
To those her most beloved, those
    Who, when she strikes with her wings,
Stand rooted, turned into a rose
    By terrestrial understandings.

Come, sulking woman, bare as water,
Dazzle me now as you dazzled me
When, blinded by your nudity,
I saw the sex of the intellect,
The idea of the beautiful.
The beautiful to which I, later,
Gave only mistrust and neglect,
The idea no dishonour can annul.

Vanquished aviatrix, descend
Again, long-vanished vision whom
I have not known so long, assume
Your former bright prerogative,
Illuminate, guide and attend
Me now. O living vision, give
The grave, the verity; and send
The spell that makes the poem live.

I sent a letter to my love
In an envelope of stone,
And in between the letters ran
A crying torrent that began
To grow till it was bigger than
Nyanza or the heart of man.
I sent a letter to my love
In an envelope of stone.

I sent a present to my love
In a black-bordered box,
A clock that beats a time of tears
As the stricken midnight nears
And my love weeps as she hears
The armageddon of the years.
I sent my love the present
In a black-bordered box.

I sent a liar to my love
　　With his hands full of roses
But she shook her yellow and curled
Curled and yellow hair and cried
The rose is dead of all the world
Since my only love has lied.
I sent a liar to my love
　　With roses in his hands.

I sent a daughter to my love
　　In a painted cradle.
She took her up at her left breast
And rocked her to a mothered rest
Singing a song that what is best
Loves and loves and forgets the rest.
I sent a daughter to my love
　　In a painted cradle.

I sent a letter to my love
　　On a sheet of stone.
She looked down and as she read
She shook her yellow hair and said
Now he sleeps alone instead
Of many a lie in many a bed.
I sent a letter to my love
　　On a sheet of stone.

O long-haired virgin by my tree
　　Among whose forks hung enraged
A sexual passion not assuaged
　　By you, its victim—knee to knee,
Locked sweating in the muscled dark
　　Lovers, as new as we were, spill
The child on grass in Richmond Park,
　　The cemetery of Richmond Hill.

Crying,the calf runs wild among
  Hills of the heart are memories:
Long long the white kiss of the young
  Rides the lip and only dies
When the whole man stalks among
  The crosses where remorse lies—
Then, then the vultures on the tongue
  Rule empires of white memories.

Legendary water, where, within
  Gazing, my own face I perceive,
How can my self-disgust believe
  This was my angel at seventeen?
Stars, stars and the world, seen
  Untouched by crystal. Retrieve
The morning star what culprit can
  Who knows his blood spins in between?

Move backward, loving rover, over
  All those unfeathered instances
I tar with kiss of pitch, the dirty
  Lip-service that a jaded thirty
Renders its early innocences.
  Pointer of recollection, show
The deaths in feather that now cover
  The tarry spot I died below.

What sickening snot-engendered bastard
  Likes making an idiot of himself?
I wish to heaven I had mastered
  The art of living like a dastard
While still admiring oneself.
  About my doings, past and recent,
I hear Disgust—my better half—
  "His only decency's indecent."

Star-fingered shepherdess of Sleep
Come, pacify regret, remorse;
And let the suffering black sheep
Weep on the bed it made. Let pause
The orphic criminal to perceive
That in the venue of his days
All the crimes look back and grieve
Over lies no grief allays.

Sleep at my side again, my bride,
As on our marriage bed you turned
Into a flowering bush that burned
All the proud flesh away. Beside
Me now, you, shade of my departed
Broken, abandoned bride, lie still,
And I shall hold you close until
Even our ghosts are broken-hearted.

So trusting, innocent, and unknowing
What the hazards of the world
Storm and strike a marriage with,
We did not hear the grinders blowing
But sailed our kisses round the world
Ignorant of monsters and the vaster
Cemetery of innocence. This wreath
Dreams over our common disaster.

But bright that nuptials to me now
As when, the smiling foetus carried
Rose-decked today instead of tomorrow,
Like country cousins we were married
By the pretty bullying embryo
And you, my friend: I will not borrow
Again the serge suit that I carried
Through honey of moon to sup of sorrow.

Loving the hand, gentle the reproving;
Loving the heart, deeper the understanding;
Deeper the understanding, larger the confiding
For the hurt heart's hiding.

26

Forgiving the hand, love without an ending
Walks back on water; giving and taking
Both sides become by simple comprehending:
Deeper the love, greater the heart at breaking.

4

O BISHOP Andrewes, Bishop Berkeley,
    John Peale Bishop and Bishop's Park,
I look through my ego darkly
    But all that I perceive is dark:
Episcopally illuminate
    My parochial testaments
And with your vestal vested vestments
    Tenderly invest my state.

Let Grace, like lace, descend upon me
    And dignify my wingless shoulder:
Let Grace, like space, lie heavy on me
    And make me seem a little older,
A little nobler; let Grace sidle
    Into my shameful bed, and, curling
About me in a psychic bridal,
    Prove that even Grace is a darling.

The moon is graceful in the sky,
    The bird is graceful in the air,
The girl is graceful too, so why
    The devil should I ever care
Capitulating to despair?
    Since Grace is clearly everywhere
And I am either here or there
    I'm pretty sure I've got my share.

Grace whom no man ever held,
　　Whose breast no human hand has pressed,
Grace no lover has undressed
　　Because she's naked as a beast—
Grace will either gild or geld.
　　Sweet Grace abounding into bed
Jumps to it hot as a springald—
　　After a brief prayer is said.

Come to me, Grace, and I will take
　　You close into my wicked hands,
And when you come, make no mistake,
　　I'll disgrace you at both ends.
We'll grace all long throughout the night
　　And as the morning star looks in
And blanches at the state we're in—
　　We'll grace again to be polite.

For Marriage is a state of grace.
　　So many mutual sacrifices
Infallibly induce a peace
　　Past understanding or high prices.
So many forgivenesses for so many
　　Double crossings and double dealings—
I know that the married cannot have any
　　But the most unselfish feelings.

But the wise Church, contemplating
　　The unnatural demands
That marriage and the art of mating
　　Make on egoists, commands
We recognize as sacramental
　　A union otherwise destined
To break in every anarchic wind
　　Broken by the temperamental.

Off the Tarpeian, for high treason,
    Tied in a bag with a snake and a cock,
The traitor trod the Roman rock.
    But in the bag, for a better reason,
The married lovers, cock and snake,
    Lie on a Mount of Venus. Traitor
Each to each, fake kissing fake,
    So punished by a betrayed creator.

"The willing union of two lives."
    This is, the Lords of Justice tell us,
The purpose of the connubial knot.
    But I can think of only one
Function that at best contrives
    To join the jealous with the jealous,
And what this function joins is not
    Lives, but the erogenous zone.

I see the young bride move among
    The nine-month trophies of her pride,
And though she is not really young
    And only virtually a bride,
She knows her beauties now belong
    With every other treasure of her
Past and future, to her lover:
    But her babies work out wrong.

I see the bridegroom in his splendour
    Rolling like an unbridalled stallion,
Handsome, powerful and tender,
    And passionate as an Italian—
And nothing I could say would lend a
    Shock of more surprise and pride
Than if I said that this rapscallion
    Was necking with his legal bride.

I knew a beautiful courtesan
    Who, after service, would unbosom
Her prettier memories, like blossom,
    At the feet of the weary man:
"I'm such a sensitive protoplasm,"
    She whispered, when I was not there,
"That I experience an orgasm
    If I *touch* a millionaire."

Lying with, about, upon,
    Everything and everyone,
Every happy little wife
    Miscegenates once in a life,
And every pardonable groom
    Needs, sometimes, a change of womb,
Because, although damnation may be,
    Society needs every baby.

It takes a sacrament to keep
    Any man and woman together:
Birds of a forgivable feather
    Always flock and buck together:
And in our forgivable sleep
    What birdwatcher will know whether
God Almighty sees we keep
    Religiously to one another?

I have often wondered what method
    Governed the heavenly mind when
It made as audience to God
    The sycophant, the seaman sod,
The solipsist—in short, men.
    Even the circus-stepping mare
Lifts her nose into the air
    In the presence of this paragon.

For half a dozen simple years
    We lived happily, so to speak,
On twenty-seven shillings a week;
    And, when worried and in tears,
My mercenary wife complained
    That we could not afford our marriage,
"It's twice as much," I explained,
    "As MacNeice³ pays for his garage."

I entertained the Marxian whore—
    I am concerned with economics,
And naturally felt that more
    Thought should be given to our stomachs.
But when I let my fancy dwell
    On anything below the heart,
I found my thoughts, and hands as well,
    Resting upon some private part.

I sat one morning on the can
    That served us for a lavatory
Composing some laudatory
    Verses on the state of man:
My wife called from the kitchen dresser:
    "There's someone here from Japan.
He wants you out there. As Professor.
    Oh, yes. The War just began."

So Providence engineered her
    Circumstantial enigmas,
And the crown of the objector
    Was snatched from me. In wars
The conscientious protester
    Preserves, as worlds sink to force,
The dignified particular.
    Particularly one, of course.

"The hackneyed roll call of chronology"—
  Thus autobiography to De Quincey.
And I can understand it, since he
  Lived like a footnote to philology.

But the archangelic enumeration
  Of unpredictable hejiras—
These, with a little exaggeration,
  I can adduce for my admirers.

And so, when I saw you, nightmare island,
  Fade into the autumnal night,
I felt the tears rise up for my land,
  But somehow these tears were not quite
As sick as when my belly laughed
  Remembering England had given me
The unconditional liberty
  To do a job for which I starved.

5

ALMIGHTY God, by whose ill will
    I was created with conscience;
By whose merciful malevolence
    I shall be sustained until
My afflictions fulfil
    His victories; by whose dispensation
Whatever I have had of sense
    Has obfuscated my salvation—

Good God, grant that, in reviewing
    My past life, I may remember
Everything I did worth doing
    Seemed rather wicked in pursuing:
Grant, Good God, I shall have remitted
    Those earthly pleasures beyond number
I necessarily omitted,
    Exhausted by the ones committed.

Good God, let me recollect
    Your many mercies, tall and short,
The blousy blondes, the often necked,
    And those whom I should not have thought
Given wisely to me; nor let forget
    My grateful memory the odd
Consolers, too frequently brunette,
    Who charged me for your mercies, God.

Good God, let me so recall
    My grave omissions and commissions
That I may repent them all,
    —The places, faces and positions;
Together with the few additions
    A feeble future may instal.
Good God, only mathematicians
    Consider Love an ordinal.

Good God, so wisely you provided
    The loving heart I suffer with,
That I am constantly divided
    By a deep love for all beneath
Me. Every man knows well
    He rides his own whores down to hell,
But, good God, every knackered horse
    Was, originally, yours.

Good God, receive my thanksgiving
    For all the wonders I have seen
(And all the blunders in between)
    In my thirty-odd years of living.
I have seen the morning rise
    And I have seen the evening set—
Anything different would surprise
    Me even more profoundly yet.

Good God, receive my gratitude
    For favours undeserved: accept
This truly heartfelt platitude:
    You gave me too much latitude
And so I hanged myself. I kept
    Your mercy, Good God, in a box
But out at midnight Justice crept
    And axed me with a paradox.

O loving kindness of the knife
    That cuts the proud flesh from the rotten
Ego and cuts the rotten life
    Out of the rotten bone! No, not an
Ounce of sparrow is forgotten
    As that butchering surgeon cuts
And rummages among my guts
    To succour what was misbegotten.

I confess, my God, this lonely
    Derelict of a night, when I
And not the conscious I only
    Feel all the responsibility—
(But the simple and final fact
    That we are better than we act,
For this fortunate windfall
    We are not responsible at all)—

I confess, my God, that in
    The hotbed of the monkey sin
I saw you through a guilt of hair
    Standing lonely as a mourner
Silent in the bedroom corner
    Knowing you need not be there:
I saw the genetic man had torn a
    Face away from your despair.

I confess, my God, my Good,
    I have not wholly understood
The nature of our holiness:
    The striking snake errs even less
Not questioning; the physicist
    Not asking why all things exist
Serves better than those who advance a
    Question to which life's the answer.

But, O my God, the human purpose,
    If at all I can perceive
A purpose in the life I live,
    Is to hide in the glass horse
Of our doubt until the pity
    Of heaven opens up a city
Of absolute belief to us,
    Because our silence is hideous

And our doubt more miserable
    Than certainty of the worst would be.
Like infinitely pitiable
    Ghosts who do not even know
They waver between reality
    And unreality, we go
About our lives and cannot see
    Even why we suffer so.

I know only that the heart
    Doubting every real thing else
Does not doubt the voice that tells
    Us that we suffer. The hard part
At the dead centre of the soul
    Is an age of frozen grief
No vernal equinox of relief
    Can mitigate, and no love console.

Then, O my God, by the hand
    This star-wondering grief takes
The world that does not understand
    Its own miseries and mistakes
And leads it home. Not yet, but later
    To lean an expiated head
On the shoulder of a creator
    Who knows where all troubles lead.

6

I LOOKED into my heart to write.
　　In that red sepulchre of lies
I saw that all man cherishes
　　Goes proud, rots and perishes
Till through that red room pitiless night
　　Trails only knife-tongued memories
To whose rags cling, shrieking, bright
　　Unborn and aborted glories.

And vinegar the mirages
　　That, moaning they were possible
Charge me with the unholy No.
　　The unaccomplished issue rages
Round the ringed heart like a bull
　　Bellowing for birth. But even so
Remorselessly the clock builds ages
　　Over its lifeless embryo.

Ruined empire of dissipated time,
　　Perverted aim, abused desire,
The monstrous amoeba cannot aspire
　　But sinks down into the cold slime
Of Eden as Ego. It is enough
　　To sink back in the primal mud
Of the first person. For what could
　　Equal the paradise of Self-love?

The necessary angel is
      The lie. Behind us, all tongue splayed,
The lie triumphant and tremendous
      Shields us from what we are afraid
Of seeing when we turn—the Abyss
      Giving back a face of small
Twisted fear—and this is all,
      To conquer the lie, that we possess.

Come, corybantic self-delusion,
      And whisper such deceptions to
Me now that I will not care who
      Or what you are, save palliation
Of the question-marked heart. Let rest
      The harp and horror horned head upon
That green regenerative breast
      By whose great law we still live on.

Now from my window looking down
      I see the lives of those for whom
My love has still a little room
      Go suffering by. I see my own
Stopped, like a stair carpet, at this story
      Not worth the telling. O memory
Let the gilded images of joys known
      Return, and be consolatory!

Bitter and broken as the morning,
      Valentine climbs the glaciered sky
With a spike in his foot. The lover's warning
      Blazes a sunrise on our misery:
Look down, look down, and see our grey
      And loveless rendezvous, Valentine:
Fold, then, in grief and cast away
      The love that is not yours or mine.

On this day of the innocent
    And happy lovers, let me praise
The grotesque bestiary of those
    Who love too much. Monsters invent
Monsters, like babies that gypsies raise
    In odd bottles for freak shows—
These love too deeply for the skin.
    Whose bottle are you monster in?

The grotesque bestiary where
    Coiled the pythoness of sighs,
To keep a beast within her there
    Crushes him in her clutch of vice
Till, misshapen to her passion, dead,
    The lion of the heart survives
By suffering kisses into knives
    And a spiked pit into a bed.

Stand in your sad and golden-haired
    Accusation about me now,
My sweet seven misled into life.
    O had the hotheaded seaman spared
Those breast-baring ova on their bough,
    There'd be no aviary of my grief,
No sweet seven standing up in sorrow
    Uttering songs of joy declared

Of joy declared, as birds extol
    The principle of natural pleasure
Not knowing why. Declare to all
    Who disbelieve it, that delight
Naturally inhabits the soul.
    I look down at you to assure
My sense of wrong: but you declare
    Whatever multiplies is right.

I looked into my heart to write.
　　But when I saw that cesspit twisted
With the disgusting laws that live
　　In royal domination under

The surface of our love, that writhe
　　Among our prizes, they attested
The putrefaction of our love
　　Spoils the spawner of its grandeur.

7

TODAY the twenty-sixth of February,
  I, halfway to the minute through
The only life I want to know,
  Intend to end this rather dreary
Joke of an autobiography.
  Thirty-five years is quite enough
Of one's own company. I grow
  A bit sick of the terrestrial stuff

And the celestial nonsense. Swill
  Guzzle and copulate and guzzle
And copulate and swill until
  You break up like a jigsaw puzzle
Shattered with smiling. The idiotic
  Beatitude of the sow in summer
Conceals a gibbering neurotic
  Sowing hot oats to get warmer.

Look on your handwork, Adam, now
  As I on mine, and do not weep.
The detritus is us. But how
  Could you and I ever hope to keep
That glittering sibyl bright who first
  Confided to us, perfect, once,
The difference between the best and the worst?
  That vision is our innocence.

But we shall step into our grave
    Not utterly divested of
The innocence our nativity
    Embodies a god in. O bear,
    Inheritors, all that you have,
    The sense of good, with much care
Through the dirty street of life
    And the gutter of our indignity.

I sense the trembling in my hand
    Of that which will not ever lower
Its bright and pineal eye and wing
    To any irony, nor surrender
The dominion of my understanding
    To that Apollyonic power
Which, like the midnight whispering
    Sea, surrounds us with dark splendour.

Enisled and visionary, mad,
    Alive in the catacomb of the heart,
O lonely diviner, lovely diviner, impart
    The knowledge of the good and the bad
To us in our need. Emblazon
    Our instincts upon your illumination
So that the rot's revealed, and the reason
    Shown crucified upon our desolation.

You, all whom I coldly took
    And hid my head and horns among,
Shall go caterwauling down with me
    Like a frenzy of chained doves. For, look!
We wailing ride down eternity
    Tongue-tied together. We belong
To those with whom we shook the suck
    And dared an antichrist to be.

Get rags, get rags, all angels, all
    Laws, all principles, all deities,
Get rags, come down and suffocate
    The orphan in its flaming cradle,
Snuff the game and the candle, for our state
    —Insufferable among mysteries—
Makes the worms weep. Abate, abate
    Your justice. Execute us with mercies!

BOOK II

1

I TURN from resting on my morals
  —So few, so faded at my brow
You'd think the wretched things were laurels—
  To summon to these puny verses
All the truths I do not know
  So that their vacant universes
May multiply, like a row
  Of empty glasses or God's mercies.

The trouble with our blood and state
  Is, simply, our state's rather bloody:
I know of no soul that can mate
  With anything but anybody.
Yet all the true soul really wishes
  Transcends the fleshpots of the skin
And even though Sex is delicious
  Would rather kith its own kin.

I sit beside the Colosseum
  Reflecting on the Christian myth:
Follow those Saints? But I can't see 'em,
  And I've got eyes to see 'em with.
No, on these ancient altars died
  Not so much as one little martyr.
But who's to tell? And what's it matter?
  All postulants are satisfied.

It is extremely difficult
 To make a lion eat a man.
These wretched beasts have one fault:
 You have to train 'em, if you can,

 To swallow human attributes.
  Somehow the lion does not savour
Our salt of the earth. These crude brutes
 Only consume us as a favour.

Also the Heraclitean fires
 For human flesh have little taste:
Cremation, even of Jews, requires
 A Gomorrahan holocaust.
And I could enumerate, tin by tin,
 If my memory were surer
The Sodoms of fuel it took to in-
 cinerate the former Führer.[4]

Are the Gods with us? They are not.
 And I do not know where they are.
Have they migrated very far?
 Can we pursue them with a rocket?
What, has the Ideos gone quite mad
 Not to be frightened of the Atom?
I hear its joke, both rude and bad:
 "Sir, it was I split the Adam."

The cave of Origins is blocked.
 The skull grins like a victory wreath
And the crossed bones underneath
 Declare that we must die for us.
Now who by who, my God, is mocked?
 The three old crones sneer at the fuss
With which we slit our esophagus
 And stand around still, looking shocked.

I saw the smooth prestidigitator
    Lifting up his bloody hands
Cry out: "Hey, folks! The Stigmata!
    It's all done with rubber bands!"
I saw the Saint lift up his hands
    Like suns over the prestidigitator
And whisper: "The wound understands.
    It divines its creator."

Not much has happened, since I sat
    By an old mill in an Essex field
Twelve years ago, and began what
    I now confess better concealed:
(Have not the Powers with their pity
    Covered over the bones of our misery?)
Not much has happened, save the Dies Irae
    Dawning on Saint Augustine's City.

2

THE little singing birds upon
    The branches of the Golden Tree
Persist in whistling on and on
    Although they are as good as dead.
The birds are silent in Italy
    But not because they are afraid:
No, for this simple reason: it
    Is hard to sing upon a spit.

As overhead our Ixion[5]
    Turns on the bright transfixion
Of the juggernauting stars
    Whose blood and thunder will
Grind us under the big Mill.
    And who shall circumvent the years
That count us down and down until
    At last a grain of carbon roars?

The hunstmen are up in America.[6]
    The fireworks of Canaveral
Celebrate Cape Carnival.[7]
    Is it a Saturnalia?
On the vast shore of Eternity
    The boys play patiently with fire,
And all the birds of Elmer Gantry[8]
    Rise to Apocalypse, or higher.

But let's not bore ourselves to death.
  (It's such a British way to die.)
There's still a joker underneath
  The royal flush of a last trump sky.
Astrology assured us just

  Exactly three brief weeks ago[9]
The Day of Wrath was here at last.
  And so it is, for all I know.

Let us assume that we are dead.
  (Yes, and you too, my feathery friend.)
With this simple-minded fiction
  We can circumvent our end,
And, as ghosts, from bed to bed
  Migrate without moral sanction,
Adamsdropping on every Eve
  A love that we need not believe.

Mock on, mock on, Gabriel, Gabriel.[10]
  What else the eyes for, save to weep?
What else the heart for, save to burn?
  What else the spirit for, save to die?
How can the tongue ever tell
  Those secrets the heart cannot keep
Without withering in its turn
  Down to the roots of sanctity?

But there, in its lovely valley
  Roams that lamb lost from the breast
And all its whickering will really
  Never lead it back to rest;
For, when the heart expects it least
  Overnight that innocence
Ages into a questing beast
  Among the rocks of existence.

Thus I record the birth of a son.
      Who dare pursue the unborn babe
Over its paradise and drag down
      That cherub howling and kicking on
The mercy of Salvador Mundi,[11] like
      A child chained to a falling globe?
It is not for that infant's sake.
      Who dare pursue the unborn babe?

The Roman couples kissing in
      The Gardens of the Giulia[12]
Do they know the maze they're in?
      A maze? A mess. Conversely, are
These turtle doves, like ageing lags,
      Delighted by the bolt and bar?
What lovelock better than the legs?
      What prison fitter than the skin?

Thus I confess the death of the heart.
      That shabby paraphernalia
The instruments of the memory
      To this obituary I bring.
The clouds of burning Carthage part,
      The willow queens prepare to sing,[13]
The heart, in its soap opera—
      Well, is it really necessary?

And so, not in silence, but apart, I
      Seek to venerate in the grove
Of implacable Astarte[14]
      The shattered trophies of that love
No sacrificial dedication
      Can sustain, and no heart
Torn on its tossed horns of union
      Ever entirely forgive.

What, to the ceremonies of despair,
    Save this oblivion can we bring:
The opiates of memory?
    But there's no poppy in that field
I lie down in: nor is there
    Oblivion in that bitter spring
That rises from our philosophy.
    Where is the wound of Memnon healed?[15]

Here on the pearled[16] rocks[17] of Rome
    I watch the Leonine City lie
At last at rest along a dream,
    And only the Tiber petering by.
So may the mind sequestered seem
    To sleep among its haunted vaults,
And never a wraith flittering home
    Perturb what no more life exalts.

3

THE five hundred and seventy-five
    Christian churches of the Eternal
City (including the Maternal and
    Magisterial Vatican)[18]
Not only keep the faith alive
    (What did the Abbé do? Survive?)[19]
But every Catholic (come and see it)
    Manages his little Fiat.[20]

Yet sometimes I see my immortal soul
    Lying underneath that tree—
O how I wish I was my soul
    And my immortal soul was me!
Then I'd lie all day long and whet
    My wings upon the Holy Missal,
But since I'm not immortal, yet,
    I'll just sit here and wet my whistle.

The Sacred Cows are lowing on
    The sunset pastures of the Convent;
The Holy Willies[21] of Salvation
    Line up to watch the Day of Judgment.
Who cried Stale Ichthus?[22] All at sea
    The fishermen drag from its bed
Our fish and chipped divinity,
    The Pilot of the Swinging Lead.

The spirit of John Henry Newman
    —That Catholic gentleman with a lamp—
Leads me with his light through Roman
    Hecatombs of the Christian Cause:
But all I find down in those damp
    And Conscience-haunted corridors
Is the white shrine of his grace
    Shining over those dark floors.

The Grammar of Divine Assent:
    I hear its silence everywhere
As metaphysical discontent
    Gibbers like a Gibbon here.
And though we howl our Yes aloud
    Out of the dirt and detritus,
Its echoes are the only word
    Of Assent that responds to us.

Dear Word and Syntax of Mankind
    Remit our sentence. Over
The contradictions undefined
    And the huge confusions may
Even a cipher, one fine day,
    Reach us all, and for ever.
And O in our extreme distress
    Permit that message to be Yes.

In the tantrums of the screaming
    Child of darkness may there not
Linger some far-off abstract dreaming
    Of the parents it has lost?
What of the Night, O Newman? What
    Of the Dark Midnight of the Soul?
Even though our star is crossed
    It's not Saint John in this Black Hole.[23]

O Red Cardinal, intercede
   For us in our greater need
Until the heavenly powers heed
   Our unavailing cry.
And O holy Henry Newman
   Declare that every man and woman
Being really only human
   Is afraid to die.

And therefore, Prince, the human station
   Itself precludes true resignation
As from the depths of our desolation
   Nightly we faltering call.
So, scarlet prelate, silver author,
   Advocate, Orator, and Father,
Permit one word. O tell us whether
   Our cry is heard at all.

For, Father, once, I, a child, alone,
   Stood looking up with reverence at you
Where, near gardens, your stone statue
   (How could you have a heart of stone?)
Smiling as though the smile would christen
   Cogitates by the Oratory.[24]
So, Prince Spiritual, not to me
   But to a child lean down and listen.

It is not, truly, out of despair
   The guilty cry, nor is it their
Intemperate desire to hear
   What they most wish were so:
No, Father. It is, truly, when
   We believe, like Tertullian,[25]
What seems impossible. O then,
   Yes, then we cry to know.

4

An Augustinian anarchist
    (Nothing can deflate the proud
Who know the worst is really best;
    That to the privileged Elect
Every damned thing's allowed
    Since they're fated to be right
No matter which side they select,
    Because they really are the Light:)

An Augustinian anarchist
    (By both horns I take the bull
Only to find that I have missed
    The golden head of the rational
In between 'em. I see that brow
    Huge where the contradictions meet
Knotted on them like a great
    Figurehead of the mental prow:)

An Augustinian anarchist
    I sit playing on the psalter
Hymns about the Antichrist
    Underneath Bernini's altar.[26]
Altar? Why, that wretched pun
    Betrays me like an open letter,
For everything I've ever done
    Should have been done a little better.

The will of man is double-headed
    Like a monster of Siam
So that, once that I have said it,
    I doubt the simple truth: I am.

There by a consoling river
    Inconsolable Janus strays
As fall and will fall for ever
    The four tears from that double face.

Which ought to be the first? To know
    Or praise? I will seek by praise.
Calling, shall I find that to call
    Is, as Hippo[27] lived to show,
The birthcry of belief? He says
    We have had declared to us
That Faith, after all the fuss,
    Finds itself in the oddest ways.

Those that speak most are most dumb.
    Who speaks for me? The poem speaks.
I confess, Rhetorician,[28] I'm
    At heart one of those moral freaks
Not satisfied that they exist
    Until they make a noise in rime.
But then, He's dumb most of the time,
    My heavenly ventriloquist.

Not that any normal man,
    Considering the enormity
Of a purpose without pity
    (And we all hope we're normal) can
Feel anything but a trifle glum
    At the Manager's malfeasance
Now we're left, for his good reasons,
    Hanging in a vacuum.

I confess, with little shame,
    Whoring after comic gods
Like the one with a chicken's name
    Apollo[29] (whom, against all odds
I found a true one, all the same)
    Or that voluptuous female whom
I approach at periods,
    Venus, barmaid of the womb.

To Hippo I came, yes, burning
    With abominable passions
Seeking, since I'm fond of learning,
    The latest in erotic fashions:
I feel, myself, a bit dejected
    —After several wives and what not—
To find that it is now expected
    I should love the Hottentot.

My mother saw that I was dead.
    I saw this also. Not just saw,
I knew it, I believed it: for
    As I lay there in my bed
I saw her like a shade that said:
    You walk up and down, my son,
And think that I am lying dead.
    Wake up, my son, if you can.

How can I wake? The time is near
    When the huge jokes mop and mow
And each one with a red-eyed tear
    Like a ruby with no glow
Hanging from an empty socket
    Cries aloud: O let us sleep!
Shut O shut the grave and lock it
    So that no one hears us weep!

How can I sleep? That night is soon
    When there is no Northern Star
And no beneficent moon
    Bright for us wherever we are.

60   I mean that midnight when we must
    No matter what we have done
Turn the eye inward and see dust
    Like Lot's wife standing by the bone.

5

BITE, bite on the holy irony
    My little soul, like a teething ring.
And when, the veil of all things drawn,
    The worlds dispersed, and the harmony
Of Heaven halleluiahing,
    When, then, hosannahed on its throne,
I see, like the Word of God declared,
    The formula Love $= MC^2$:[30]

Bite, bite on the holy irony!
    O microscopic instrument
Of the inward-visioned eye
    All that you think that you see
You do not see, for we invent
    Out of the heart afraid to die
The Avatars of the conscience,
    The Molochs of Eternity.

The viper and his generation
    Cry out with tears of fire for
One hieroglyph, as on the rock
    Of our spiritual dereliction
We gnaw our own guilt and expire.
    Hear, hear our hissed ejaculation
Sigh up among the rocks! The snake
    Burns in its own tears like a lake.

The viper cries out for its god.
    Here in these lines, above all
I seek to praise as best I may
    And even though the viper's brood
Might hiss and whisper in this way
    I praise the intellectual
Inaccessibility
    Of the Logos Spiritual.

If not to me, since not to me
    The sunburst Logos, like a prize
Turns and flashes at my eyes
    But, like the lightning in a cloud
Appals with what I cannot see:
    Yet some, with second sight endowed,
Have heard and seen in Moses' tree
    The fiery Paraclete chant aloud.

As I have trod that flying vault
    La Verna of the bleeding cave:[31]
Dark, like a calm of waters, felt
    That ragged saint walking the wave
Of human violence; even held
    Those roses that grow without a thorn
Where, stricken by his Christ, he knelt,
    The man who drew blood out of stone.[32]

Because the intellect, self-defiled,
    Defiles its own environment,
It is O is it only to those
    —The fallible saint, the gullible child
And all things that are innocent
    Whatever does not know it knows
To whom the X-ray vision's sent—
    The Word asleep under the Rose?

"In dreams responsibilities
  Begin." So whispered Yeats in a dream.
And in the locked womb where they sleep
  Until, from that atrium
They drag the babe to Kingdom Come,
  The sacred moral verities—
Those origins of our martyrdom—
  Sew the whirlwinds that we reap.

O Love, keep those oracles warm
  In seed and hymeneal bed:
It takes a Samson to get born,
  All men are martyrs when they're dead.
For, Love, the Virgins of Desire,
  Those engines of the god's descent,
Carry within, like hanging fire,
  His unborn image immanent.

6

THE greatest of the Irish lyres
    (Not bards I speak of, but of harps)
That lovely lyre of Brian Boru
    Whose silence buried Ireland's hopes,
Muted these last two hundred years
    Today in Bloomsbury once again
Sang the last time.[33] And I will too,
    Just once, and strike my liar then.

How to pursue the trade of poet
    When, like that harp, the system dies,
The heartstrings wither, and the spirit
    Rots as its sickness falsifies
The harmonic mind until it's mute.
    It is not time alone decays
The hand we harp with, but the wind
    That plays upon the unstrung mind.

This wind, zephyring to the west,
    Wrings such wild chords and broken themes
From foregone aims, forfeited times,
    From Lorelei who will not rest:
We are the instruments of these dreams
    Possessed by the dispossessed
Like ghost hamlets, home from home,
    Haunted by what we loved the best.

Is there no solace in that hand
    That sweeps across us to elicit
Lyrical response? That thundering anger
    Not only sunder the chord, but mend?
What's the Medusa's cunning? Is it
    She blinds us only to the danger?
The consolations of song visit
    No consolations on the singer.

Thus the old apple of the heart
    Rots and the ravening crows peck at it
Till from the core emerges what it
    Seems a bit flattering to call Art.
This aftermath, like thought, is grass,
    The parasite of a dying body;
Thus all the Arts are as morbid as
    A necrological study.

That bed, it is a bed of thorn.
    Who can rest there? As we lie
Tossing and turning in the night
    Up through the soul then, like a horn,
Grow the conceptions, which, in turn,
    Yield roses as their causes die:
The rose burns in the eye; the eye
    Waters the roses as they burn.

How can we speak of what is gone
    Save from that dead end into which
The very violence and passion
    Of our love has driven us? Speech
Serves little purpose, surely, when
    Alone within our dereliction
The voice has no one else to reach
    And no word not a contradiction.

"Essex gave me birth, and Sex
    Death. I lie here, poet
Of hawkers, bottles and bad cheques." [34]
    I paraphrase the Mantuan's great
Masculine memorial.
    For through its heroic spirit speak
And echo from a cloudy peak
    The clarions of Roncesvalles. [35]

The Castle of San Angelo
    That rules the Tiber like a crown
With its winged angel brooding down
    Over two thousand years below:
So, over heroic dedication
    Either to idea or action
Reigns that angel who always dies,
    The seraph of self-sacrifice.

And in our historiography
    The word upon the mountain drives
Through spiritual geography
    Upward as the hero lives.
And therefore, in an abstract sense
    The excelsiors of the mind
Emulate the heroic kind
    On Matterhorns of intelligence.

I see Smart,[36] gibbering, in a cave
    Kneeling where no goat would; at
A crevasse in the icebound soul
    Cowper sits imbibing tea:[37]
Pound whistling in an iron cage
    Over an avalanche; Eliot
Roping down an untamed gale,
    And old Yeats, frozen in majesty.

George Byron, limping in a storm
    Born from his breast, coronet
Cast to the winds; the hunchback form
    Clambering like a marmoset
Up the great peaks, the little Pope;
    Poor discalced Clare,[38] an eidelweiss
Caught in his hand instead of rope,
    Trapped in madness as in ice.

Catullus with an icicle
    Driven through his heart; old Blake
Like a bald prophet on a tricycle
    Riding the Trinity; Leopardi[39]
Crouched in Recanati like
    A bat; the good guide Thomas Hardy
Lost in vast mist; and the metaphysical
    Fury assaulting them all alike.

At the Pythian tabernacle
    Those who immolate themselves before
The altars of the syllable
    Challenge her Image to appear,
She whose gift is the vocable
    To those who die to amuse her,
The divine undying Sybil
    With the head of a Medusa.

O Golden-mouthed Catechumen[40]
    Who taught you how to raise
For the hero of the human
    Our word against the gale, our praise,
Our Chrysostom Golden Tongue
    Hung flickering like a bright Amen
On silence where no stars have sung:
    Christening with a phrase!

7

In the Abyss, the big Abyss
        Hear all creatures rejoicing
As old Circe the Pythoness
        Binds us all in illusions:
Hear one and all together voicing
        Such delight in these delusions
That the babe smiles on the spit
        At Mercy smiling opposite.

The lion thinks that he is free
        As, goaded by the golden chain
Of his impassioned spirit, he
        Is driven like a hurricane
Destroyed by its own energy.
        And thus the hero and the martyr
Born in the fires of their nature
        Cry out to burn again.

By Babylons and Jerusalems
        Wherever the heart is hung
So lost in a fever of bad dreams
        That their nightmare Exile seems
Like deserts on the tongue:
        Those, those who reach the Jordan water
Find, as they lean down, the streams
        Of Mercy boiling like a crater.

Where shall we find a little love?
    (No, not that jigged hugger-muggering
The rubber of the monkey shove,
    The bouncing and the buggering:
Not the jacked ripper of the hip
    That dies in sighs and leaves a sorrow
Every man's stiff upper lip
    Appeases twice again tomorrow:)

Where shall we find a little love?
    The dying moon of the human heart
Seeming to look down from above
    Does not, but circles as a part
Of the common or garden dance
    Moving like a dove around
Her cage of man in observance
    Of that love where both are bound.

The denser mantle of the globe
    —She wears her seas as Hermione
Of Lakedaemonia split the robe,[41]
    Or as Pamphilia to Pliny—[42]
This denser mantle, like the veils
    The Nike of Samothrake
Strikes forward through, only reveals
    The Orphics of her secrecy.

Matrix. O Mater Gloriosa
    Whom man and beast and all
Creatures that move in her circle
    Their earthly paradise call,
Fold, fold to your bosom closer
    The Beast of the Golden West
That, raving through the zodiacal,
    Leaves only a fouled nest.

8

A CARDINAL shrank from reading Saint Paul
    For fear of spoiling his style;
I shrink from writing this stuff for fear I'll
    Find there's nothing in it to spoil.
Which might be delightful for you, my dear,
    (Why don't you slip out for a drink?)
But if I weren't scribbling this drivel here,
    Why, bless me, I'd have to think.

And never a man I ever knew
    Could take his head in his hand
And think himself out of the juicy stew
    In which, to the neck, we stand.
Yes, my friend, not only I, but you
    Boil in the cannibal pot,
For the lot of man is a fiery brew,
    So skoal. And don't think a lot.

(And I've still got half the blasted
    Stuff to add yet to all this.
Well, half bested's half wasted:
    What arf ain't, Hafiz, arf is.[43]
No matter how fine may be the *finis*
    Or how staggering the start,
Whatever happens in between is
    Just to keep the two apart.)

You tender and charitable vine
    Bending your summer arbour
Over the peasant and his wife
    As, resting from their labour,
They see, like a country dance in the wine,
    Their long domestic bridal,
So, over all who marry life,
    Bend tenderly your idyl.

Especially extend to those
    My peers, the poets, whom
You receive some honour from
    As each one, whistling, goes
Down the dark stairway, to them give
    In the cold-blooded crisis
At least the illusions of your love,
    Ithyphallic Dionysus.

And of these, in particular, two,
    (A lick, as it were, and a promise)
Louis MacNeice and Dylan Thomas
    Poets who thoroughly well knew
The bending elbow learns to lean
    Upon the midnight writing table
A little firmer if it's been
    Taught to steady the unstable.

Or that deaf poet whom the fishy
    Girls upon their ragged rock
Chant vainly to, and close their ears
    Knowing that his poems make
A furious silence out of theirs—
    Does he ever lie and wish he
Never heard his silence break
    To their incommunicable airs?

O laurelled and bullroaring boy
    Who brought my cup from India
No less I intercede for one:
    (And by one, yes, I mean my
First person not so singular)
    Extend to me, and not alone,
Those liberties the lost enjoy
    In loving cup and loving eye.

And so, upon jackanapes and jackass,
    The ageing shades and the bereft,
Pour out your libation, Bacchus,
    Until not a drop is left;
As we our spirit also render
    Oblative and rather flighty
To Apollo the Avenger
    And appalling Aphrodite.

9

TODAY, the 26th of February
 Nineteen hundred and sixty-two
(Exactly twelve years to the very
 Day I started to review
This never really necessary
 Sentence I hard-labour through)
I hope to end the sorry story
 And find something nice to do.

I record the death of love.
 Allow that derelict house to stand
Abandoned where such gardens were
 As now the undergrowth and creeper
Hesitate to weave and wave
 Where love was. Let adder and
Fang of remorse never stir
 My dream and solitary sleeper.

In that old cottage with a well
 So full, now, of dead love like leaves
Where, bound within each other's spell
 We two shared our lucky lives:
Under the shoulder of that Black Hill [44]
 Old Tennyson ruled on, there we nursed
That love whose dying is the worst
 Because we believe it never will:

O wounded Eros! Those twelve
 Now burnt and gutted years around
Us lifted up their veils of fern
 And hid us from all save ourselves
Like two survivors in a wood.
 There such a secret we had found
Within that shabby farm of Hearne
 As neither of us understood.

But on that Black Hill breeds the adder—
 Bright in the dusk he shines, and shakes
Old Adam's tree of the bad apple:
 I hear him smiling as he strikes.
I took, as to a family breast
 That fork-legged hisser by the door:
I watched her falling in the west.
 Cassiopeia, rise no more.

Those twilight landscapes, hill and field
 Darkened and livid, house and tree
In their own weirder shade concealed,
 The slash of shark-white in the sky
Where a dead heaven lies revealed,
 Speak with a posthumous voice to me:
"What can the day do, save to die?
 Or human love, save cease to be?"

Yes, it is later than I think.
 Not evening shades me, but that hour
When we see the light at last
 Fallen in ruin on the west.
In that first total dark, distinct
 As a dead moon might rise and show a
Cemetery of the mind, I feel
 Only the past henceforward real.

That biology of seven sevens
    I celebrate on this bitter day
Brings to the mysteries of living
    A greater mystery, which is this:
There is a kind of hope, even
    Though no Shepherd's Evening may
Transfigure it, which, giving
    Forgiveness, gives us all there is.

Therefore to contemplate, by the sea
    By the long summer sea, the shouting
Child old Wordsworth also saw[45]
    The son of my ashes brings to me
Delight in which there's little doubting
    As, like a porpoise by the shore,
Those beautiful generations ride
    In victory on the immortal tide.

My little son, my little son,
    As pretty as a cherry
Blow on the conches once again
    Like any other cherub:
Although at morning from the leaf
    The lachrymae of the sky
As softly fall as the stars of grief
    At evening from your eye.

My little son, my little son,
    No hand will bar the door.
How can the darkness enter in
    With such a brightness there?
For, from that infant and wild face
    Innocence, outraged, stares:
This is the anger of our grace
    No god, or demon, dares.

10

No, not in that resignation
  Which, like the spectre of dead faith,
Wanders all ways because it's blown
  By consciousness of its own death:
But in the hopeless act of faith
  That, with eyes closed, and lying down,
Mourns on the grave from which it's flown:
  This dead dog is my moral wreath.

Death before death. The sun is split.
  Snakes of intellect, swarmed in a chain,
Chant the abomination of dawn.
  Sterile and blind, the great sea turtle
Weeps for us, and we weep for it.
  By Aphrodite's tortured myrtle
A monstrous Eros, blind again,
  Lies aborted and stillborn.

How can the living Word declare
  After the formal murder of
God at the hand of Robespierre
  The degradation of that Idea
Lying dead across the sky?
  Was this a suicide of Love?
Ah, did he cry out loud "Enough!"
  The Moses over Sinai?

Mary, three white mandrills sat[46]
    Under a mushroom tree in the cool
Of the evening picking slowly at
    The fleck of eye left in the skull
And the soiled morsel of the Good
    Still stuck within the marrowbone.
And there they squat, the Three in One,
    The Shapes of Man, the Apes of God.

Liberty, and every man should know,
    Is, as old Duns Scotus said,
The knowledge of our necessity.
    Within this serene ceremony
Creatures of all circumstance
    Know that they follow or are led
In perfect patterns as they go
    Dovetailed in their obedience.

Like the Huron Prince who saw
    The broken totem and prescience
Of doom written on the future tense
    Ordaining the destruction of his nation:
Then led them down to the lake shore
    And walked before them into the wave;
And there, in that glittering resignation,
    This people found a grave.

11

THEY will not come again, the days
    Auroral Anadyomene[47]
Rose whispering in the nets of praise
    From the founts of my memory.
Was it to haunt the mind misspent
    And set a memory between us
That vision in the dawn was sent
    O double-hearted Venus?

I haunt your grove, I haunt your grove
    Vae Victress[48] of my Mayday,
You who ride the crest of the grave
    And rainbow of my heyday:
I found them sleeping on the wave
    The halcyon and the skeleton;
Yet still in that bed of death and love
    They float for ever on.

Burn to the bone, eat to the soul,
    Ashes and acid of remorse;
No hero died on that hot coal.
    What hotpit ever could be worse
Than where we walked, happy my hurt,
    The Herculaneum of the heart
Together? Underneath that dirt
    May no resuscitation start.

And risen from the rivering years
     Like Ophelia she appears
Memory from whose falling stream
     Echo and lost voices seem
To rise up, calling. May no response
     Vex those spectres that spoke once:
And may no recollections gall them
     As our dead affections call them.

(Love, you Valkyrie of the bed,
     Honeytongued bitch and Clytemnestra,
The day is done and the dog's dead.
     Let the knife, as the wounds fester,
Be buried in its shrine of sores
     Until the cold incestuous cause
Secreted in a heart of ice
     Never reveals that heart is yours.)

This female with a false Truth
     Stuck in her jaw, victress of life,
The rage of age, the rage of youth,
     Love, like a gorgeous Messalina[49]
(You may imagine she's your wife,
     But Love, my friend, is even meaner),
Smiles as she parts those honey lips
     From which pure belladonna[50] drips.

The Lives of Gallant Women seem
     To come among me like a dream
Or, in spite of Alfred Tennyson,[51]
     Like a flying Spanish medicine.
This Dream of Fair Women sees
     No psycho in my psychoses:
Those seas so perilous to swim in
     Not for the sharks, but for the women.

They glide and shimmer, with their pale
    Proud bellies swelling as they find
They've got a mouthful of the male;
    But still, they leave the bits behind

Of that detesticulated diver
    Who thought to hunt the Tigress-Shark
And from the cunt, without a mark,
    Emerge, the first survivor.

The lovers lying at their ease
    Like coldblooded snakes that creep
And curl together half asleep
    Eating each other by degrees
Until these heart-shaped heads of Satan
    Stare bodiless at each other:
So, fattening as we're being eaten,
    We devour one another.

Not in our deep and mutual
    Need of Love can we confute
That we live in the incommunicable
    And lonely liberty of the brute:
Not there, but in the complicity
    Of moral treason, in the trust
Betrayed by the heart's duplicity,
    The marriage of our dust.

12

WE all know the rich love themselves
 (Might perhaps some of us love them?)
But why must they hate everyone else?
 Ah, with what a Stoic phlegm
They face the old dilemma: whether
 To lie about in bed all day
Tickling the arse with a peacock feather
 Or get up and buy Naples Bay?

"The rich *are* different," sighed FitzGerald,
 "From us." . . . But then he was a Scott.
And since the poor these days are not
 (According to the *Daily Herald*)
With us any more, O where's
 That difference which was theirs?
Society (that's us, my dear FitzGerald),
 Trembles when its classes are imperilled.

Money I loved, and, next to money, money.
 What to give the man who's got everything?
(I accept cash.) This gift's as good as any:
 To know a little touch'll bring
The Miser Midas out of a smiling friend.
 (And what the hell else, anyhow, can we spend?
Giving and taking, we lay waste our spendings.
 Yes, only cheque-books have unhappy endings.)

The retail price of peace of mind
    (I have this on the authority
Of the highly prized Ted Roethke)
    Is the sum of fifteen grand
82   (U. S. dollars) in the clear.
        And when you've got your belly full it's a
Sure sign that you've had a Pulitzer
    (Which is an Honour, not a brand of Beer.)

Three new powder blue Cadillacs
    Stood outside that festive door
(Unlike the Virgins of Bryn Mawr
    Who lay inside on their backs)
Waiting soberly for New York's
    Three great bards, whose Income Tax
(What with Professorships and perks[52])
    Filled more pages than their works.

And as we left that modest orgy
    (The poetesses had no hair
But proved their creative energy
    Like radiators, with hot air)
The poets gazed at the Cadillacs
    Muttering: "Yup. By Jeez, we'll show 'em.
Take a gander at the fax:
    All this for tossing off a poem."

What can I say? I'll say it louder.
    I show you Love in a handful of dust.
The only trouble with this powder
    Is that it's yellow, rare, and must
Like chimney sweepers, come home dirty.
    Ah, my friend, it's not Time that's Money,
Just as Faust isn't really Goethe.
    No shit—(are you?)—is worth a penny.[53]

Money is Love. Now ask me why.
 Friend, I truly needn't waste a
Half a lifetime to reply:
 Like any other poetaster
I've got the snazziest reason why.
 Let me be perfectly realistic:
To the poet and the mystic
 All is Love under the sky.

A second law of Love and Money
 (Lend me your ears, if nothing better)
Is that there simply isn't any.
 The mystic does not know Moneta
(Roman goddess of hard cash)
 Sees that we remain her debtor;
Nor, save in bed, does the *poeta*
 Ever find Love in the flesh.

The third law, and quite as funny,
 Is this: the more you have of either,
Well, the more you need the other.
 Money needs Love, and Love needs Money.
Juvenal, in his levity,
 Is, nevertheless, meticulous:
He knew his onion: poverty
 Makes any man ridiculous.

13

O MASTER of the Thorny Ways
    Hear, from the jubilant pit
The torn and tongued flesh praising it,
    Hear us, as we rejoice!
So in this verb and act of praise
    Of things that triumph as they die
I raise my token verse and voice
    And cannot question why.

For we were born—and Ignatius
    Loyola ought to know—
To praise, to reverence and to serve[54]
    —(O Task and Master!)—here below.
The reverence is in the service,
    The service, for me, in the praise:
And this is more than we deserve
    Considering our ways.

How can the I that has seen
    Apollo die in the solar web
And heard the inheritors of Job
    Wish that they had never been:
The agonized dragonfly of kind
    Broken upon an Abstract Will:
How can I look on this and still
    Speak from a heart resigned?

The diatonic intellect
      Possesses its own diapason
But the voluntary of soul
      That the hand of heaven plays on
Humankind, is so perfect
      That we cannot hear the whole,
For far beyond the reach of reason
      Roar the nearest chords of all.

Resignation, therefore, in
      Our Cloud and Tree of Unknowing
From whose groves of origin
      Birds as of Paradise and shadowing
Divinations haunt and assail us:
      We know that the Eternal Tense
Crowns the Cloud of our Ignorance
      Like an Aurora Borealis.

As lovers lie on summer nights
      By lakes whose waters shake with stars
And like twin hands around a vase
      Climb sleeping up the spellbound heights
Of Eros: so white sky and lake
      Gleam in their mysteries and seem
So deep in love they cannot wake
      At dawn's passover in the dream.

I hear the fanfares of the day
      As unveiled Asia announces
The cyclix passion of God's will
      Shake the mountains, shake the mountains
Till, like the earthquake fate of clay,
      Destiny falls in avalanches
Launched at the crack of doom, until
      Day trembles in its bright foundations.

O Master of the Scourge and Rod
    (And any honest man can learn a
Lesson like this at La Verna)[55]
    So our lives, as they descend,
Sometimes, like a rainfall, shed
    Roses, as, to serve your end,
The rods of double Justice bend
    Into a Bedlam or a bed.

O bed of roses! Let the man
    Here in the prisons of the Night
And dreaming with a second sight
    Look up to see, like Aldebaran,
The gold sunsetting mask of God
    Christening us with our day's
Apotheosizing blaze
    Like Death hanging fire overhead.

NOTES

All of the following notes are the author's unless otherwise indicated. Those marked with an asterisk, however, were written at the publisher's request, and were, in some cases, revised by the publisher.

BOOK I

[1] J. K. Huysmans, French author whose novel, *Against the Grain* (1884), celebrates a life of overrefined and homosexual esthetics.*

[2] François Villon.*

[3] Louis MacNeice (1907-1963), British poet. See Book II, 8, sixth stanza.*

BOOK II

[4] Some eighty imperial gallons: see H. R. Trevor-Roper's *The Last Days of Hitler*.

[5] In Greek legend, the king of the Lapithae who was bound to a turning wheel of fire for his impiety.*

[6] Sir Thomas Browne, *Religio Medici*.

[7] Carnival: literally, 'Farewell to the flesh.'

[8] Rockets (Cape Canaveral—now Cape Kennedy—jargon).

[9] See *The London Times*, February 16, 1962.

[10] See William Blake's poem, *Mock on, Mock on, Voltaire, Rousseau*. Gabriel, the first Messenger of God, is traditionally supposed to be the only archangel who can speak. See Book II, 1, seventh stanza, 'Now who by who, my God, is mocked.' (I am aware that this is ungrammatical, but I think it sounds better than "who by whom.") *

[11] The name of a maternity hospital in Rome. Also, the World's Saviour.

[12] These gardens, in the Roman Forum, are much favoured by lovers.*

[13] Dido, Queen of Carthage. 'Dido with a willow in her hand'—Shakespeare, *The Merchant of Venice*, V, i. This hysteric burned down Carthage and died in the flames when Aeneas, like a sensible man, abandoned her.*

[14] Astarte, the Phoenician goddess of fertility and reproduction. Her grove in Carthage was notorious for its orgies. See Flaubert's novel, *Salammbô*.*

[15] A reference to the hole in the throat of the Colossus of Memnon, through which, at dawn, a wind off the Nile blows and produces a very sad howling. This sound was once thought to be the voice of the god. Memnon = Memory. The voice of memory = poems. The wound of Memory = those griefs that occasion certain poems.*

[16] Pearl = Paul.

[17] Rock = Peter. Both saints were martyred in Rome.

[18] *Mater et Magistra*, title of encyclical by Pope John XXIII.

[19] See the Abbé Sieyès (1748-1836), French abbé, statesman, and theorist of the revolutionary and Napoleonic era. He renounced his faith and survived politically by frequently shifting his position. When asked what he did during the Revolution, he replied: 'I survived.' [Publisher's Note]

[20] Vatican pronunciamento. Also popular Italian automobile.

[21] See *Holy Willie's Prayer*, poem by Robert Burns.*

[22] Ichthus = fish (in Greek). Also sacred name of Christ from the initial letters of the Notarica: *I*esous *CH*ristos, *TH*eou *U*ios, Soter: Jesus Christ, son of God, Saviour.

[23] *The Dark Night of the Soul* is the title of a poem by St. John of the Cross. The Black Hole is the Black Hole of Calcutta in which over one hundred Europeans were crushed and suffocated to death at the start of an Indian mutiny in 1756.*

[24] The Brompton Oratory, London.

[25] Tertullian, early Christian writer: 'I believe because it is impossible.' *

[26] The High Altar at St. Peter's, Rome, designed by Bernini.*

[27] St. Augustine (354-430), bishop of Hippo.

[28] Augustine was, at one time, a teacher of rhetoric at Milan.

[29] I know this is unpardonable, but I like it because it's absurd. Apollo = a *pollo* (Italian for chicken).*

[30] Einstein's formula, Energy = MC^2.*

[31] St. Francis received the Stigmata at a cave in La Verna. There is now a chapel there called the Chapel of the Stigmata.*

[32] At Portiuncula, Assisi, where he threw himself on roses, they now grow without thorns. At this place there now stands the Chapel of Roses.*

[33] See *The London Times*, February 16, 1962.

[34] 'Mantua gave me birth, Calabria death. I lie here, poet of shepherds, farms and heroes'—Virgil's Epitaph.

[35] The horn of the Paladin Roland blown at the pass of Roncesvalles.*

[36] Christopher Smart (1722-1771), British poet, author of *Rejoice in the Lamb,* was certifiably nuts.*

[37] William Cowper (1731-1800), British poet, was subject to fits of mania and depression. [Publisher's note]

[38] John Clare (1793-1864), British poet, was a farm boy and died insane. When he was asked how he wrote his poems he said, 'I went out into the fields and found them there.' Discalced means barefooted or shoeless. See Order of the Discalced or Poor Clares, Roman Catholic nuns.*

[39] Giacomo Leopardi (1798-1837), born in Recanati, was almost blind.*

[40] St. John Chrysostom (c.345-407), [Chrysostom = Golden Tongue], early bishop of Constantinople, was a convert—hence catechumen, one receiving religious instruction prior to baptism. [Publisher's note]

[41] A whore mentioned in one of Sophocles' plays.

[42] 'That woman Pamphilia ought not to be deprived of one jot of her glory, that of having invented a dress which exhibits a woman perfectly naked'—Pliny, the Younger.

[43] This is the most atrocious pun. What half ain't, Hafiz, well, half IS. It is done in Cockney. The poems of the Persian poet Hafiz are notorious for their suggestibility.*

[44] Blackdown, Sussex, where Tennyson died, after a residence of many years.*

[45] 'And see the children sport upon the shore

And hear the mighty waters rolling evermore'

—from Wordsworth's *Ode on the Intimations of Immortality.**

[46] See T. S. Eliot's *Ash Wednesday*.

[47] Anadyomene = foam-born. Epithet of Venus. She was born from the foam that rose when the testicles of her father were chucked into the sea.*

[48] Simply: Woe to the Victress.*

[49] Roman Empress and whore, or, conversely, whore and Empress—wife of Claudius.*

[50] The poison, deadly nightshade. It also means "beautiful woman" in Italian.*

[51] See Tennyson's poem, *A Dream of Fair Women. The Lives of Gallant Women* refers to a book by Abbé Brantôme (Pierre de Bourdeille). The 'flying Spanish medicine' is cantharides or Spanish fly, an aphrodisiac.

[52] Perquisites.*

[53] Still the price for the use of a public urinal in Britain.

[54] 'Man was born to praise, reverence and serve God.' Opening sentence of the Spiritual Exercises of St. Ignatius Loyola.

[55] See Book II, 5, sixth stanza.